Irish Wit

**Look out for these other titles
from Des MacHale:**

Wit
Wit Hits the Spot
Wit on Target
Wit – The Last Laugh
Wit Rides Again
Wisdom

and coming soon:

Ultimate Wit

Irish Wit

Des MacHale

MERCIER PRESS

First published in Ireland 2002
Paperback edition published in 2005
Mercier Press
Douglas Village
Cork
www.mercierpress.ie

Copyright © Des MacHale 2002

A catalogue record for this book is available
from the British Library.

ISBN 1 85635 461 X

Cover design by Grade Design Consultants

Typeset by E-Type

Printed in Great Britain
by Mackays of Chatham Ltd, Chatham, Kent

Contents

Liam Fay • David Feherty • Ray Fitzgerald

Pat Fitzpatrick • Donal Foley • Joe Foyle

Neil Francis • Percy French • Greer Garson

Stan Gebler-Davis • Kevin Gildea • Alice Glynn

Oliver St. John Gogarty • Oliver Goldsmith

Philip Greene

Eoin Hand • Richard Harris • Michael Hartnett

Neil Hassett • Charles Haughey • Father Healy

Maurice Healy • Jackie Healy-Rea • Noel Henderson

George Hook • John Hume

James Joyce • Nora Joyce

Robert Kane • Patrick Kavanagh • Eamon Keane

John B. Keane • Roy Keane • Charles Kelly

Eamon Kelly • James Kelly • Edward Kenneally

Mary Kenny • Declan Kilberd

Hugh Leonard • C. S. Lewis • Desmond Lynam

Declan Lynch • Robert Lynd

Patrick MacGill • Des MacHale • Dominic MacHale

Mícheál MacLiammóir • Seumas MacManus

Seán MacReamoinn • William Maginn • John P. Mahaffy

Count Mahoney • Leslie Mallory • Edward Martyn

Father Mathew • Kevin McAleer • Mary McAleese

Donal McCann • Mick McCarthy • Barry McGuigan

Benny McHale • Jack McHale • Sammy McIlroy

James McKeon • John McKeowan • Ginger McLoughlin

Frank McNally • Spike Milligan • Sean Moncrieff

Christy Moore • George Moore • Patrick Moore

Thomas Moore • Dylan Moran • Eamon Morrissey

Andy Mulligan • John A. Murphy • Thomas Myles

Eamon Nally • Michael Neary

Conor Cruise O'Brien • Daire O'Brien

Edna O'Brien • Flann O'Brien • Vincent O'Brien

Ken O'Callaghan • Phil O'Callaghan • Brendan O'Carroll

Sean O'Casey • Daniel O'Connell • Michael O'Connell

Frank O'Connor • Joseph O'Connor • Jimmy O'Dea

George O'Dowd (Boy George) • Sean O'Faolain

Sian O'Gorman • Ardal O'Hanlon • Maureen O'Hara

Kevin O'Higgins • Brendan O'Mahony • Eoin O'Mahony
Alfred O'Rahilly • Liam O'Reilly • Tony O'Reilly
Shamus O'Shamus • Peter O'Toole

Ian Paisley • Charles Stewart Parnell • Maureen Potter
Sarah Purser • Pat Rabbitte • Michael Redmond
John Reidy • Albert Reynolds • Boyle Roach
Hal Roach • George Russell

George Salmon • George Bernard Shaw
Jim Sheridan • John D. Sheridan
Richard Brinsley Sheridan • Fergus Slattery
James Stephens • Jonathan Swift • J. M. Synge

Dennis Taylor • Niall Toibín • Joe Tomelty
Eric Tully • George Tyrrell

Mervyn Wall • Tony Ward • Duke of Wellington
Oscar Wilde • John Winstanley • Gordon Wood

John Butler Yeats • William Butler Yeats

What They Say about the Irish

Rowan Atkinson • Jo Brand • George Carlin

Quentin Crisp • J. P. Donleavy • Kenneth Fraser

Sigmund Freud • Oliver Herford • Samuel Johnson

Sidney Littlewood • Patrick Murray • Austin O'Malley

Eugene O'Neill • Jeff Probyn • Will Rogers

Barry Took • Mark Twain

The Irish have a reputation for being the wittiest people on earth and when you read this book you will soon see why. Wit drops from the lips of the average Irishman and Irishwoman as naturally and as frequently as rain drops from the heavens on the Emerald Isle. Pick up any book of quotations in the English language and you will find it chock-full of quotations from Irish authors such as Wilde, Shaw, Sheridan (R. B. and J. D.), Swift, Behan, Milligan, Beckett, Keane, O'Brien, Toibín, Leonard, Goldsmith, Joyce, Healy, Kavanagh, MacManus, Mahaffy, Moore, O'Casey, O'Faolain and Stephens. That's a formidable list by any standards. And these are just the literary wits that have left a written record of their humorous outpourings. Go to any Irish pub, golf club, school, football match, office block or factory floor, and you will hear just as good stuff, off-the-cuff and original too. What causes it and where does it come from? God only knows and He must bear at least some of the responsibility because He is probably part Irish Himself. Maybe it is something in the air, something in the water, something magic that exists in the Irish twilight between sanity and madness. Whatever the reason, let us rejoice in it and enjoy one of the world's greatest free gifts – Irish humour.

Des MacHale, 2002

Joseph Addison

Why should we do anything for posterity?
What has posterity ever done for us?

Her grief lasted longer than I have ever known
any widow's – three days.

They were a people so primitive they did not
know how to get money except by working for it.

Bertie Ahern

I will not upset the apple tart.

Dave Allen

My church accepts all denominations – fivers,
tenners, twenties.

My bank manager went for a heart transplant but they couldn't find a stone of the right size.

White is the virginal colour, symbolising purity and innocence. Why do nuns wear black?

If I got as much as £3,000 of a night's work I could do an impression of Paul Getty counting his small change.

Irish humour consists of five basic themes – life, death, religion, drinking and the English.

I'm an atheist, thank God.

Ireland has one of the world's heaviest rainfalls. If you see an Irishman with a tan, it's rust.

Ireland is the only place in the world where procrastination takes on a sense of urgency.

My favourite retort to hecklers is, 'If I had a head like yours, I'd have it circumcised.'

Parents say things like 'Would you like a smack?' and 'I'll teach you to be disobedient.'

Samuel Beckett

Dublin University contains the cream of Ireland – rich and thick.

We are all born mad. Some remain so.

I am not British. On the contrary.

There are only two moments worthwhile in writing; the one when you start and the other when you throw it in the wastepaper bin.

Brendan Behan

New York is my Lourdes, where I go for spiritual refreshment – a place where you are not likely to be bitten by a wild goat.

The drink in that pub is not fit for washing hearses.

There is no bad publicity, except an obituary notice.

When I came back to Dublin I was court-martialled in my absence and sentenced to death in my absence, so I said they could shoot me in my absence.

Kilbarrack, over by Howth, my father always maintained, was the healthiest graveyard in the country, with the sea air.

People don't actually swim in Dublin Bay
– they are merely going through the motions.

The first item on the agenda of every Irish organisation is 'The Split'.

How about the raffle where the first prize was a week in Belfast and the second prize was a fortnight in Belfast?

Critics are like eunuchs in a harem; they know exactly how it should be done – they see it being done every night, but they cannot do it themselves.

I have never seen a situation yet so bad that a policeman couldn't make it worse.

A job is death without the dignity.

Here's to the harp of old Ireland, and may it never want for a string as long as there's a gut in a peeler.

Cork people would steal the cross from behind Jesus' back and leave Him hanging in mid-air.

Yes we do have a bath in the house
– but thank God we've never had to use it.

The Irish Navy is the best in the world. Every evening all the sailors can cycle home for their tea.

The best words any man can hear at his funeral are 'Carry on with the coffin. The corpse'll walk.'

The day the Catholic and Protestant Churches combine, it's the end of all drinking. I'll have to go to Rome and sabotage the affair.

A drama critic has the same effect on me as a bicycle without a saddle.

I would be going against my religion if I drank tea or coffee.

I gave him a Ringsend uppercut
– a kick in the groin.

The wolf would never come to my door. He knows I'd drag him in and eat him.

My cousin Jimmy Burke was the only one who could write. I mean his name.

The best thing I can say about bagpipes is that they don't smell too.

He was shot in the Dardanelles, a very painful spot to be shot in too.

My granny lived on tinned salmon, snuff and porter and never got out of bed except for funerals.

Brian Behan

A party was thrown in Hollywood in 1966 for the wrap-up of the Marlon Brando film *A Countess from Hong Kong*. The film was such a flop, it was suggested they should dump the film and release the party.

I am giving up marriage for Lent.

My brother Brendan was the sort of man who would get a panic attack if he saw someone wearing a teetotaller's badge.

Dominic Behan

Then one day they opened a Catholic chapel, which was followed by a pub, a block of shops and eventually a school. The school went up last because there was no profit in it.

They say the altar wine contains Glauber's salts so as priests won't get the taste and break their pledges.

Kathleen Behan

I wouldn't trust my husband with a young woman for five minutes, and he's been dead for twenty-five years.

The neighbours said to me, 'Oh, Mrs Behan, don't go out to Kimmage – that's where they eat their young.'

Stephen Behan

If you have money spend it. First on necessities such as drink, and then if there is anything left over, on food, shelter and clothing.

George Best

I am attending Alcoholics Anonymous, but it's difficult to remain anonymous.

I've stopped drinking. But only while I'm asleep.

In 1971 I was sent off the field for arguing with one of my own team-mates.

In 1969 I gave up drinking and sex. It was the worst twenty minutes of my life.

Some of my friends said they didn't think I behaved too badly on Wogan. Like Alex Higgins and Oliver Reed for example.

It's a pleasure to be standing up here. In fact, it's a pleasure to be standing up.

I used to go missing a lot – Miss Canada, Miss United Kingdom, Miss World.

Just my luck to have given up drinking when the pubs are staying open all night.

George A. Birmingham

This book is dedicated to any friend I have left in Ireland after its publication.

He lied like an eyewitness.

Danny Blanchflower

The secret of football is to equalise before the opposition score a goal.

Dion Boucicault

How I wish that Adam had died with all his ribs in his body.

Elizabeth Bowen

Edith Sitwell is like a high altar on the move.

Tony Butler

The management of an Irish pub cannot be held responsible for any accidents which occur in the mad rush for the doors at closing time.

The Irish climate is wonderful, but the weather ruins it.

In Ireland when the weather forecast is bad, it's invariably correct; when it's good, it's invariably wrong.

Gabriel Byrne

Never work with children or Denholm Elliot.

Patrick Campbell

From my earliest days I have enjoyed an attractive impediment in my speech. I have never permitted the use of the word 'stammer'. I can't say it myself.

In New York it would be absolutely magical if we could alleviate our hunger with something that tasted of food.

The only people I've ever given working orders to have been occasional charwomen, and mostly I've told them not to bother, that I'd do it myself.

My back swing off the first tee put the pro in mind of an elderly woman of dubious morals trying to struggle out of a dress too tight around the shoulders.

Golf is the only game in the world in which a precise knowledge of the rules can earn you a reputation for bad sportsmanship.

Roddy Carr

When I roomed with Simon Hobday in South Africa he designated Monday as washday. That meant filling a bath with water, pouring in a liberal amount of detergent, emptying in the entire contents of his suitcase and then proceeding to stir the lot with a putter. When he felt the clothes had been stirred sufficiently, they were thrown out on the balcony to dry.

Edward Carson

My only great qualification for being put at the head of the Navy is that I am very much at sea.

Frank Carson

I was standing beside this fellow in a bar in Belfast and I said to him, 'You're not from round here, are you?' 'No,' he replied, 'but how on earth did you know that?' 'You just left your drink down,' I said to him.

My favourite item from an Ulster newspaper went like this: 'Man and woman wanted to look after two cows, both Protestant.'

Knocking down a house in Dublin recently, the workmen found a skeleton with a medal on a ribbon round its neck. The inscription was Irish Hide and Seek Champion, 1910.

Murphy did the 100 metres in record time. He got six months – they were gas meters.

In the pole vault Cassidy did twenty feet but he was disqualified. He didn't come down.

Last time I performed, my name was so low on the programme I was getting orders for the printing.

This Scottish fellow had a hip replacement operation. He asked the surgeon if he could have the bone for the dog.

These two Irishmen were passing a pub – well, it could happen.

I used to sell furniture for a living. The trouble was, it was my own.

Three ducks were flying over Belfast. The first duck said 'quack', the second duck said 'quack' and the third duck said, 'Look, I'm going as quack as I can.'

The difference between my wife and a terrorist is that you can negotiate with a terrorist.

I'm not really a homosexual – I just help them out when they're busy.

My brother has an unusual job. He finds things before other people lose them.

Michael Clifford

You cannot throw a stone in Ireland without hitting someone who thinks he's an intellectual.

Pádraic Colum

The ideal marriage consists of a deaf husband and a blind wife.

Paddy Crosbie

If bullshit was music, that fellow would be a brass band.

Danny Cummins

I don't normally sing and when I sing I don't sing normally.

John Philpot Curran

My dear doctor, I'm surprised to hear you say that I am coughing very badly, because I have been practising all night.

When I can't talk sense, I talk metaphor.

Trevor Danker

Found guilty of embezzling £5,000, Mr Thanes Nark Phong, a hotel cashier from Bangkok, had his sentence reduced from 865 years to 576 years because 'his testimony proved useful'.

Elias Mutumbe, a Kenyan forger, has been jailed for three years after issuing a series of high value banknotes bearing his own likeness.

Michael Davitt

You are not a proper member of an Irish club until you are barred.

Terence de Vere-White

De Valera discloses the workings of a mind to which incoherence lends an illusion of profundity.

James Dillon

My family was in Irish politics while De Valera's was still bartering budgerigars on the back streets of Barcelona.

Aubrey Dillon-Malone

Have you heard the one about the Irishman who joined Alcoholics Anonymous? He still drinks but under a different name.

Patrick Doherty

I took a job as a postman. It doesn't pay much but it's better than walking the streets.

Denis Donoghue

The only function of a student at a lecture is to be present when a great mind communes with itself.

Roddy Doyle

They would have been working class if there was any work.

James Duffy

Thrifty! Man, she'd skin a flea for his hide.

Joseph Duffy

There is a fierce smell of plutonium in many
Dublin public toilets.

Argentina is a true democracy – everybody
eventually becomes President.

Myles Dungan

If David Feherty hadn't been a golfer he probably
would have been a wringer-outer for a one-armed
window cleaner.

James Dunne

The quiet Irishman is about as harmless as a
powder magazine built over a match factory.

Maria Edgeworth

A naturally free, familiar, good-natured, precipitate Irish manner had been schooled and schooled late in life into a sober, cold, stiff deportment which she mistook for English.

John Eglington

Carleton was a man sent by God in response to the general clamour for an Irish Walter Scott.

Liam Fay

When they made Carrie Crowley, they threw away the mould. But some of the mould grew back.

As an effective means of communicating complex arguments, the television discussion programme ranks somewhere between smoke signals and interpretative dance.

I tune into antiques programmes only to savour the expressions on the faces of the grasping old codgers who have just heard that the cobwebby pile of tat they have been hoarding under the bed for half a century is actually a cobwebby pile of tat after all and not a voucher to be cashed in for a trough of loot that could in turn be hoarded under the bed for another half century.

David Feherty

My golfing partner couldn't hit a tiled floor with a bellyful of puke.

Colin Montgomerie has the temper of a warthog recently stung by a wasp and a face like a bulldog licking piss off a nettle.

John Daly's divots were travelling further than my drives.

Eamon Darcy has a golf swing like an octopus falling out of a tree.

In my singles match I saw Hope vanishing over the horizon with her arse on fire.

I was swinging like a toilet door on a prawn trawler.

Ballesteros spends so much time in the woods that he carries an axe as one of his clubs.

Colin Montgomerie is a few fries short of a happy meal. His mind goes on vacation and leaves his mouth in charge.

John Daly has the worst haircut I've ever seen in my life and I've seen a few bad ones. It looks like he has a divot over each ear.

Colin Montgomerie couldn't count his balls and get the same answer twice.

Ray Fitzgerald

How would you know if your goldfish was incontinent?

Pat Fitzpatrick

On ringing a restaurant to ask if they had wheelchair access I was told that they accepted all major credit cards.

Donal Foley

A fine soft day is a day of incessant rain accompanied by a force nine gale.

Though not a formally religious man, he never darkened a church door in his life.

His charity was legendary: he subscribed to the Herald Boot Fund, 1921.

He was a devoted family man: he spent Christmas Day at home.

Dublin was a clear winner in Bord Fáilte's 'Dirty Towns' competition. The strong smell of the Liffey, with its fascinating tang of urine, excreta, rotten dogs and decayed fish, sent Dublin into an unassailable lead.

The Dáil has a valuable therapeutic function insofar as it keeps a number of potentially dangerous men off the public streets.

Joe Foyle

The Protestant Churches look after you from birth to death; the Catholic Church looks after you from conception to resurrection.

Neil Francis

What James Dalton lacks in intelligence, he makes up for in stupidity.

Percy French

I have just returned from a children's party. I am one of the survivors. There are not many of us.

Greer Garson

Why do I not like Marlon Brando? Because I don't enjoy actors who seek to commune with their armpits.

Stan Gebler-Davis

Irish weather consists of rain – lots of it. It has
been known for the rain to cease sometimes for as
much as two weeks at a time. But when this
happens the Irish complain of drought, pestilence
and imminent bankruptcy.

The Race Relations Board concentrated their fire
some years ago on a man who was selling Irish
Coffee mugs which had the handle on the inside.
He turned out to be a native of Cork.

Kevin Gildea

I bought an audio cleaning tape. I'm a big fan of
theirs.

Brevity is the.

My mum and dad are both dead and now I think of some of the things I wish I'd said to them, like 'Be careful of that bus.'

Alice Glynn

A woman voting for divorce is like a turkey voting for Christmas.

Oliver St. John Gogarty

William Orpen never got under the surface until he got under the sod.

I'm told Bernard Shaw went to church the other day and when they passed him the collection plate he moved aside murmuring 'Press'.

When St Patrick first visited Ireland there was no word in the Irish language to express sobriety.

Newgrange is described as a pre-Christian cemetery, but this would be misleading except to us who know that the question of subsequent Christianity is unfounded. There is no such thing as a large whiskey.

If Evan gave all his reasons for joining the Catholic Church he would be excommunicated.

Oliver Goldsmith

On the stage David Garrick was natural, simple, affecting. It was only when he was off that he was acting.

The man recovered of the bite,
The dog it was that died.

I am told he makes a very handsome corpse and becomes his coffin prodigiously.

There is nothing so absurd or ridiculous that it has not at some time been said by some philosopher.

The wise are polite all the world over, but only fools are polite at home.

Phillip Greene

His doctor told him to avoid excitement so now he watches only League of Ireland football matches.

Eoin Hand

There are only two inevitable things in life – people die and football managers get sacked.

Richard Harris

I am in God's departure lounge and I've managed to miss quite a few scheduled flights.

I've formed a new group called Alcoholics Unanimous. If you don't feel like a drink, you ring another member and he comes over to persuade you to go to the pub.

I've got to stop talking Viagra because I can't zip up my trousers.

Michael Caine is an over-fat, flatulent, 62-year-old windbag, a master of inconsequence now masquerading as a guru, passing off his vast limitations as pious virtues.

Michael Hartnett

There are three mythical figures in Ireland – Cúchulainn, Fionn MacCumhaill and 'just the one'.

The most brilliant people I know have been in institutions. I worry about the ones who haven't. There is no certificate of sanity for them.

English is the perfect language to sell pigs in.

Neil Hassett

There are just three certainties in life – death, taxes and television repeats.

Charles Haughey

I have done the public. Some service! And they know it.

Father Healy

I would prefer Heaven for climate but Hell for society, as all my friends are Protestants.

Lunch is a poor compliment to breakfast and an insult to dinner.

Maurice Healy

You may leave the court with no other stain on your character than the fact that you have been acquitted by a Limerick jury.

Religion is not involved in this case, m'lud. All the parties concerned are Presbyterians.

Jackie Healy-Rae

Who are the plain people of Ireland? They are the people who have their dinner in the middle of the day.

Noel Henderson

The present state of English rugby is serious but not hopeless; the present state of Irish rugby is hopeless but not serious.

George Hook

Being hit by Victor Costello is like being hit by a cement mixer travelling at forty miles an hour.

Scotland are the nymphomaniacs of world rugby.

John Hume

If the word 'No' was removed from the English language, Ian Paisley would be struck speechless.

The truth is that Ulster Unionists are loyal not to the Crown but to the half-crown.

Anyone who isn't confused in Northern Ireland doesn't really understand what is going on.

James Joyce

You may certainly not kiss the hand that wrote *Ulysses*. It's done lots of other things as well.

Become a Protestant? Certainly not. Just because
I've lost my faith doesn't mean I've lost my reason.

I am a strict teetotaller, not taking anything
between drinks.

Nora Joyce

James, why don't you write books that people can
read?

If only James had stuck to music, we might have
made some money.

I always told James that he should give up writing
and take up singing.

Robert Kane

Signor Angeli, Professor of Italian at Trinity College, Dublin, was asked to translate the proceedings of the opening of Queen's College, Cork into Italian and forward them to the Pope. He reported the fact that the ceremony was attended by both men and women as 'there were present men of both sexes', which led a cardinal to observe that Cork must be a very queer city.

Patrick Kavanagh

I was a genius and therefore unemployable.

I have been friendly with Brendan Behan only in the hope that I would be free from the horror of his acquaintanceship.

I have lived in poverty for twenty years in the illiterate and malignant wilderness that is called Dublin whose inhabitants care nothing for the things of the spirit. They blathered about poetry but they knew as much about it as my arse knows about snipe shooting.

In Dublin you are worse off if you have written books than if you are illiterate.

I never refuse money. I come from a family where it was considered unlucky to refuse money.

The best thing I ever wrote was a cheque for £5,000 that didn't bounce.

There are over thirty words in the Irish language which are equivalent to the Spanish 'mañana'. But somehow none of them conveys the same sense of urgency.

There is something wrong with a work of art if it can be understood by a policeman.

The trees along the banks of the Royal Canal are more sinned against than sinning.

I have just returned from a trip to Paris and let me tell you, lads, courting in Monaghan is only in its infancy.

Eamon Keane

The fulminations of the missionaries about sex in Listowel will have as little effect as the droppings of an underweight blackbird on the water level of the Grand Coulee Dam.

John B. Keane

There he goes – the man what learned me English.

He is such a devout Catholic, he won't be happy until he is crucified.

Given the unlikely options of attending a funeral or a sex orgy, a true Irishman will always opt for the funeral.

The ultimate role of the Catholic Church in Ireland is the propagation of bingo.

I once knew a woman who wore out three bicycles in search of a cure for corns.

I was entering a hostelry in Killarney when I was approached by a man who accused me of never having written about bucket handles.

I have no objection to long tedious plays. I always feel fresh when I wake up at the end.

In the book of records Dandy Keane was credited with landing the largest enamel chamber pot ever to be hooked by rod and line from one end of the Feale River to the other. I have no idea how many gallons it would contain, but under the entry ran the following description: Chamber Pot. Enamel. Perforated at bottom. Handle attached. To hold the water of twenty.

Roy Keane

It was grand playing for Nottingham Forest. Brian Clough told me just to go out, get the ball and give it to my Nigel.

Charles Kelly

A modern sculptor is a man who can take a rough block of stone or wood, work on it for months and make it look like a rough block of stone or wood.

Eamon Kelly

They told me it was a bird bath but I didn't believe them. There isn't a bird alive who can tell the difference between Saturday night and any other night of the week.

'Tis always a mystery to me how women got on before the looking-glass was invented.

When they heard he was from England, they filled him up with every kind of story, for they do enjoy the like.

I knew an 85-year-old man who married a girl of 18. He wanted someone to answer the Rosary for him.

James Kelly

Never marry a widow unless her first husband was hanged.

Edward Kenneally

What is an Irishman but a mere machine for converting potatoes into human nature?

Mary Kenny

I never make the same mistake twice. I always make new ones.

Declan Kiberd

The only Irish known to R. M. Smyllie was whiskey, which he drank from a hand covered in a white glove, a consequence of a promise to his mother on her death-bed that he would 'never touch a drop again'.

Hugh Leonard

All our operators are either drunk or fornicating right now, but if you care to leave a message when you hear the tone ...

I once saw Michael Scott taking alternate sips of Scotch and Alka Seltzer, thereby acquiring and curing a hangover simultaneously.

— Daddy, when I'm grown up I want to be an actor.
— Don't be greedy son, you can't be both.

From experience, I know that anything ending in '–os' on a restaurant menu is pronounced 'heartburn'.

If you are inserting a suppository last thing at night, always take your socks off first and if you are inserting a suppository first thing in the morning always ensure that your socks are on first. Bending over can cause the thing to fly out with great velocity and there is always the danger of a ricochet. Once I broke a holy statue.

The most effective way of getting rid of vermin is hunting – provided that a sufficient number of them fall off their horses and break their necks.

There is only one immutable law in life – in a gentleman's toilet, incoming traffic has the right of way.

My grandmother made dying her life's work.

It was embarrassing. I felt like a figure skater who had forgotten to put on her knickers.

The problem with Ireland is that it is a country full of genius, but with absolutely no talent.

Never under any circumstances write comedy for laughs. This is as ruinous as believing that your wife means it when she says: 'Tell me all about her. I swear I don't mind.'

Fintan O'Toole is to theatre what bed-wetting is to nurseries.

C. S. Lewis

He that but looketh on a plate of ham and eggs to lust after it, hath already committed breakfast with it in his heart.

Desmond Lynam

If you're a sporting star, you're a sporting star. If you don't quite make it you become a coach. If you can't coach, you become a journalist. If you can't spell, you introduce Grandstand on a Saturday afternoon.

Declan Lynch

Men have walked on the Sea of Tranquillity but are still barred from walking through certain parts of Ulster.

One critic deemed *Fergus' Wedding* about as funny as an outbreak of venereal rash.

Robert Lynd

Every man of genius is considerably helped by being dead.

Patrick MacGill

God is choosy about the company He keeps and
never comes near Derry.

Des MacHale

My favourite event at the Wimbledon tennis
championships is the mixed singles.

The main reason why the Irish took to
Catholicism so easily is that it was founded by a
man who could turn water into wine.

There comes the dreaded moment in any
anthology when yours truly decides to include –
himself. This fact alone is enough to condemn the
book out of hand; if the anthologist cannot see the
huge gap between his own pathetic offering and
the others, he is obviously not fit to do the job in
the first place.

I treat homosexuals in exactly the same way as I treat everyone else – with contempt.

MacHale's Law: in any assortment of mixed biscuits, the chocolate biscuits disappear first.

Tiger Woods' idea of an up-and-down is a birdie on a par three.

The best live entertainment in Ireland is a funeral.

Albert Einstein held that nothing could move faster than light. I beg to differ. He never saw anybody reach for the TV remote control when a Party Political Broadcast comes on the screen.

Dominic MacHale

I've never had amnesia – not that I can remember anyway.

Mícheál MacLiammóir

A journalist once asked me if I had ever slept with a woman. I replied that I had been accused of being many things in my life but never of being a lesbian.

The Irish Republic tonight at midnight: Hilton Edwards piously thanked God that England was free at last from 700 years of Irish domination.

Seumas MacManus

It is bad manners to begin courting a widow before she gets home from the funeral.

Never make a task of pleasure, as the man said when he dug his wife's grave only three feet deep.

There are three things to beware of: the hoof of a horse, the horn of a bull and the smile of an Englishman.

Ballygullion girls have a dispensation from the Pope to wear the thick end of their leg downwards.

He was a man of his word and his word was no good.

Drying widows' tears is the most dangerous occupation known to man.

Seán MacReamoinn

Like the Irish Census, I am broken down by Age,
Sex and Religion.

William Maginn

The safety of women consists in one circumstance
– men do not possess at the same time the knowledge of thirty-five and the blood of seventeen.

A married woman commonly falls in love with a
man as unlike her husband as is possible – but a
widow very often marries a man extremely
resembling the defunct. The reason is obvious.

Don't marry any woman under twenty; she is not
come to her wickedness before that time; nor any
woman who has a red nose at any age; because
people make observations as you go along the
street. 'A cast of the eye' – as the lady casts it on
you – may pass muster under some circumstances;
and I have even known those who thought it

desirable; but absolute squinting is a monopoly of vision which ought not to be tolerated.

John P. Mahaffy

What the difference between a man and a woman is I cannot conceive.

In Ireland the inevitable never happens but the impossible always does.

An Irish atheist is one who wishes to God he could believe in God.

An Irish bull is always pregnant.

I am told that Traill is ill. Nothing trivial I hope.

My dear Oscar, you are not clever enough for us here in Dublin. You had better run over to Oxford.

No one ever sank to the depths of evil all at once: it takes forty years to become a Senior Fellow at Trinity College, Dublin.

Beware of French actresses, especially when you are 108.

Count Mahoney

I can understand Italian, your Majesty, if it's spoken in Irish.

Leslie Mallory

Diaries are full of indispensable information, such as recommended tyre pressures for North Korea.

Edward Martyn

George Moore suffered from mental diarrhoea
which had to be shot all over his friends.

Father Mathew

Horse sense is something a horse has that prevents
it betting on people.

Kevin McAleer

In those days the best show on television was
called Closedown – it lasted most of the night.

Is there an afterlife? Well, there's an afterbirth so
why shouldn't there be an afterlife?

My grandfather and the whole family used to sit
for hours in front of the television watching it

intently. Eventually he would say, 'Will we switch it on?'

Mary McAleese

My opponents have done a full 360-degree turn on this issue.

Donal McCann

Those whom God wishes to punish He makes mad. Then He gives them an equity card.

Mick McCarthy

People seem to think that Jack Charlton and I are exactly the same. But I was a forthright, blunt, arrogant bastard long before I ever got involved with him.

They tell me the new striker can run pretty quickly, but how fast can he limp?

Barry McGuigan

I missed Nicky Perez with some tremendous punches. The wind alone from them could have caused him pneumonia.

Benny McHale

Three little boys were each asked to put a penny in the church collection and to quote a verse from the Scriptures as they did so. The first said, 'It is more blessed to give than to receive'; the second said, 'The Lord loves a cheerful giver'; and the third said, 'The fool and his money are soon parted.'

Jack McHale

Only one part of the body must not move during an Irish dance – the bowels.

Never count your blessings before they hatch.

Sammy McIlroy

My left foot is not one of my best.

James McKeon

Mixed-faith marriages were frowned upon in Killcock. Both parents had to sign a declaration that any babies that resulted from the union had to be brought up as children.

Ever since he was a child, Paddy had wanted to be a priest, but he was refused entry into Maynooth Seminary because of his height. He wasn't able to reach up to the altar. Anyway, he could never stand all that early morning drinking.

John McKeowan

At no point in the performance of *Good Mourning, Mrs Brown* is Brendan O'Carroll in danger of becoming two-dimensional.

Ginger McLoughlin

The hardest part of my famous Twickenham try was not resisting the English pack but dragging the entire Irish pack over with me.

Frank McNally

The only constant factor of American eating competitions is the basic rule of competition 'Heave and you leave.'

My wife has a complex accounting system. She does an initial scan of the supermarket total and says, 'Oh my God!' Then she puts the receipt away carefully in a drawer with all the others which ensures that eventually we will have enough receipts to fill a box.

Spike Milligan

Deprived of my British citizenship, I rang up the Irish Embassy and asked if I could have Irish citizenship. 'Bejasus, yes,' an official replied, 'We're terrible short of people.'

A man loses his dog, so he puts an ad in the paper. The ad says, 'Here, boy.'

The first joke in my book is 'it's aardvark, but it pays well'.

We all have our hang-ups but unfortunately mine is hanging down.

At my army medical examination the doctor said to me, 'Get your clothes off.' I said, 'Shouldn't you take me out to dinner first?'

I remember once going into an undertakers', lying on the floor and shouting 'shop'.

I went to Naples to see Vesuvius and would you believe it, the bloody fools had let it go out.

I swear I once saw a road-sign in Ireland which read: Warning! This is a one-way cul-de-sac at both ends.

I have called my house 'The Blind Architect'.

I was upstairs painting a bedroom when I felt hungry, so I picked up the telephone and had the Post Office deliver a telegram to my wife downstairs asking her to send up some soup and sandwiches.

Money can't buy you happiness, but it does bring you a more pleasant form of misery.

It was the perfect Irish marriage – she didn't want to and he couldn't.

I have the body of an eighteen-year-old. I keep it in the fridge.

A sure cure for seasickness is to sit under a tree.

My father had a profound influence on me – he was a lunatic.

Sean Moncrieff

The way to beat Osama bin Laden is through humiliation. The CIA should kidnap him, give him a sex change operation and send him back to Afghanistan.

Christy Moore

I can't open my eyes when I'm singing because the words are written on the back of my eyelids.

I told the hall manager I wanted some electric fans in the wings but he told me that most of the audience came in just to see me sweat.

George Moore

All I will say about G. K. Chesterton is that he likes belching.

George Russell's only fault was his inability to distinguish between turbot and halibut.

In the pages of Pater, the English language lies in state.

Oscar Wilde paraphrased and inverted the witticisms and epigrams of others. His method of literary piracy was on the lines of the robber Cacus, who dragged stolen cows backwards by the tails to his cavern so that their hoofprints might not lead to detection.

In Ireland a girl has the choice between perpetual virginity and perpetual pregnancy.

Don't touch a woman's knee at the dinner table.
She has an instinctive knowledge whether a man
who touches her knee is caressing her or only
wiping his greasy fingers on her stocking.

I attribute my long and healthy life to the fact that
I never touched a cigarette, a drink, or a girl until I
was ten years old.

If I was to write *Diarmuid and Gráinne* in French,
Lady Gregory would then translate my French
into English; O'Donoghue would then translate
the English into Irish and then Lady Gregory
would translate the Irish into English! After that
Yeats would put style on it.

All reformers are bachelors.

The real genius for love lies not in getting into, but
getting out of love.

It does not matter how badly you paint as long as you don't paint badly like other people.

At forty-six or thereabouts one begins to feel that one's time for love is over; one is consultant rather than practitioner.

There is nothing so consoling as to find that one's neighbour's troubles are at least as great as one's own.

If there were no husbands, who would look after our mistresses?

Critics are remembered only by what they failed to understand.

They lived on money borrowed from each other.

Patrick Moore

Astrology proves at least one scientific fact – there's one born every minute.

Thomas Moore

'Come, come,' said Tom's father,
'At your time of life,
There's no longer excuse
For thus playing the rake.
It is time you should think boy,
Of taking a wife.'
'Why so it is father –
Whose wife shall I take?'

Dylan Moran

I simply refuse to countenance paintings that do not have at least a horse, gladioli or a canal in them.

Critics – the very word suggests an insect.

You walk into an estate agent's office and all the roulette tables become desks.

Eamon Morrissey

The European Parliament has banned smoking by its MEPs while it is in session. The reason is that those fellows drink so much that if you lit a match in there the place would explode.

Andy Mulligan

As the Bible says, it is easier for a rich man to get through the eye of a needle than for a camel to get into heaven.

John A. Murphy

The D-Day invasion of Normandy was very important because it saved a large part of Europe from the Russians.

During World War II, Ireland was neutral on the Allied side.

Thomas Myles

Why should Irishmen stand with their arms folded and their hands in their pockets when England called for aid?

Eamon Nally

An Irish politician is a man of few words but he uses them often.

Bord Fáilte road signs are ignorance embossed in cast iron.

There has been another revolution in South America. But then it's Tuesday, isn't it?

Michael Neary

When primitive man beat the ground with sticks, they called it witchcraft. When modern man does the same thing they call it golf.

Conor Cruise O'Brien

You are not an agnostic, Paddy. You are just a fat slob who is too lazy to go to mass.

A socialist is a Protestant variety of communist.

I have been described as a lighthouse in the middle of a bog – brilliant but useless.

Daire O'Brien

Where did I first kiss my partner? On her insistence.

I would like to die from hypothermia brought about by the breeze from my slave girls' ostrich feather fans.

Edna O'Brien

Ideally I'd like to spend two evenings a week talking to Proust and another conversing with the Holy Ghost.

Flann O'Brien

Waiting for the verb in German is the ultimate thrill.

The medical profession was not always the highly organised racket it is today.

Banking is the second oldest profession but more profitable than the oldest profession.

The right to pay fees to lawyers is a fundamental and ancient human right, and is at the kernel of what we know as democracy.

Whiskey puts a lining like leather on the stomach, a man from Balbriggan was telling me.

It cannot be too often repeated that I am not for sale. I was bought in 1921 and the transaction was final and conclusive.

It has been held that the teaching of subjects other than fishing not through Irish but through the medium of Irish leads to a generation 'illiterate in two languages'.

The typical west of Ireland family consists of father, mother, twelve children and resident Dutch anthropologist.

The brother opened Charley in 1934. He gave Charley's kidneys a thorough overhaul, and that's a game none of your doctors would try their hand at.

I know of only four languages – Latin, Irish, Greek and Chinese. These are languages because they are instruments of integral civilisation. English and French are not languages: they are mercantile codes.

The task of reviving Irish, we are told, would be hard unless conversations could be limited to requests for food and drink. And who wants conversations on any other subject?

His condition is improving rapidly – he is sitting up in bed blowing the froth off his medicine.

In Germany last year I only had to raise my hand to have my tricycle mended every day.

Vincent O'Brien

The real beauty about having Lester Piggott ride for you in the Derby is that it gets him off the other fellow's horse.

Ken O'Callaghan

An Englishman sucked his Viagra tablet instead of swallowing it. He wound up with a stiff upper lip.

Phil O'Callaghan

When I toured with the Irish rugby team I found social contact with other members of the squad very difficult. They were always using big words like 'galvanise' and 'marmalade'.

Brendan O'Carroll

When I am trying to manage the kids at Christmas, I can understand why some animals eat their young.

One Christmas things were so bad in our house that I asked Santa Claus for a yo-yo and all I got was a piece of string. My father told me it was a yo.

Sean O'Casey

I never heard him cursing; I don't believe he was ever drunk in his life – sure he's not like a Christian at all.

I'm telling you, Joxer, the whole world's in a terrible state of chassis.

P. G. Wodehouse is the performing flea of English literature.

Daniel O'Connell

He had all the characteristics of a poker except its occasional warmth.

Peel's smile is like the silver fittings on a coffin.

Michael O'Connell

When losing heavily at a game of doubles in tennis, a good ploy is to whisper to one of your opponents when changing ends, 'Your partner's playing very well.'

Frank O'Connor

The most famous building in the heart of Dublin is the architecturally undistinguished Abbey Theatre, once the city morgue and now entirely restored to its original purpose.

Joseph O'Connor

Kingsley Amis once said that sex is a great cure for a hangover, which must be the case, because if you thought Kingsley Amis was going to make love to you, you'd certainly avoid getting drunk in the first place.

Two out of five Irish women prefer alcohol to sex, and it's my luck to have gone out with both of them.

Jimmy O'Dea

Dublin snobbery – all fur coats and no knickers.

George O'Dowd (Boy George)

Madonna is a gay man trapped in a woman's body.

Sean O'Faolain

An Irish queer is a fellow who prefers women to drink.

Did it ever occur to you that the bottom of a whiskey bottle is much too near the top?

All Corkmen have a hard streak in them. The gentlest are the most cruel. All are cynics. The smilers are the worst.

A true Irishman is a fellow who would trample over the bodies of twelve naked women to reach a pint of porter.

Sian O'Gorman

Dancing at Lughnasa was widely ignored by audiences and savaged by critics much like Meryl Streep's baby was in *A Cry in the Dark*.

Ardal O'Hanlon

If I could take just two books to a desert island, I'd take a big inflatable book and *How to Make Oars Out of Sand*.

Ireland has a great reputation as a literary nation. You walk into any pub in Dublin and it's full of writers and poets. In most other countries they're called drunks.

My ambition is to host a TV chat show with Neil Armstrong and never once mention the moon.

The ancient Greek philosophers could look up at the sun and tell what time of day it was. In Ireland we never had that particular option.

Maureen O'Hara

John Ford shot a retake only if the horses had misbehaved.

Kevin O'Higgins

When I think of the hardship involved in having only seven hours to drink on a Sunday, my soul shudders.

Brendan O'Mahony

I feel like the fellow who fell into a vat of Guinness. I know exactly what to do, but where to begin?

Eoin O'Mahony

My entire involvement with the Irish Literary Revival consisted in standing beside Mr W. B. Yeats in the urinal during an interval at the Abbey Theatre, where I remember he was having great difficulty with his waterworks.

Alfred O'Rahilly

Seamus Kavanagh attempted to write a comprehensive dictionary of the Irish language but was stranded on a psychological plateau at the letter H for many years.

Liam O'Reilly

He was a good family man. Everywhere he went, he started a new family.

I slept like a baby. Every three hours I woke up looking for a bottle.

Tony O'Reilly

The voice of rugby commentator Winston McCarthy was like the love call of two pieces of sandpaper.

Before the match at Twickenham I went into the English dressing room and asked if anybody could lend me a bit of hairy twine for my boots.

Horrocks–Taylor came towards me with the ball. Horrocks went one way, Taylor went the other and I was left holding the hyphen.

Sir Christopher Dilke kept his wife in one part of a very big bed and his mistress in another, and neither knew the other was there.

Shamus O'Shamus

Cork, like Dublin, possesses a river, but there is no record that any Cork townsman has ever succeeded in spitting across it. That is not to say that the townsmen of Cork have given up trying. Indeed, some Cork townsmen endeavour to keep themselves in practice even when their beautiful river is not in sight.

A complete description of Belfast is given by: Population 200,000; early closing day Wednesday.

Peter O'Toole

I'm not crazy, but I think everyone else is.

I am the only man in the world whose first and second names are both synonyms for 'penis'.

Ian Paisley

Who is King Billy? Go home man and read your Bible.

I have reason to believe that the fowl pest outbreaks are the work of the IRA.

The RUC do not assault anyone at a republican parade unless they see fit.

The Catholics have been interfering in Ulster affairs since 1641.

In some copies of the article 'The Power of Papacy' the Pope was described as His Satanic Majesty. This should have read The Roman Antichrist.

I do not accept the word of the slanderous bachelor who lives on the banks of the Tiber.

Charles Stewart Parnell

Gentlemen, it seems unanimous that we cannot agree.

Maureen Potter

Assumpta, take your foot out of your mouth, it's a fast day.

Christy, look at the ink you've spilled on that tablecloth and your father hasn't even read it yet.

Some Irish drinkers won't take a bath unless it has a head on it.

You're not supposed to look happy doing an Irish dance.

As the Dublin woman said when she saw the Leaning Tower of Pisa, 'willya looka, it's crooka'.

Sarah Purser

Some men kiss and tell; George Moore tells but doesn't kiss.

Pat Rabbitte

Minister Michael Smith's solemn intonation is like that of a monsignor on a bad line from Medjugorje.

Michael Redmond

All these people with wooden legs – it's pathetic, they're not fooling anyone.

People often say to me, 'What are you doing in my garden?'

I like going into newsagents' shops and saying, 'Excuse me, is that Mars bar for sale?' When he says, 'Yes,' I say, 'I might be back later, I still have a few others to look at.'

And on the eighth day God said, 'OK, Murphy, you can take over now.'

Like most Irish people I was born a Catholic. This came as a big shock to my parents who were Jewish.

John Reidy

If you vote for me, not only will I return Northern Ireland to the Republic, but I'll get back Gibraltar and Hong Kong as well.

Albert Reynolds

I don't intend to write a book until Northern Ireland settles down a bit.

I haven't read a book in years – I have a big stack of them.

Boyle Roach

No man can be in two places at the one time unless he is a bird.

The man who would stoop so low as to write an anonymous letter, the least he might do is to sign his name to it.

We put them all to the sword; not a soul of them escaped alive except some that were drowned in the adjoining bog.

The only living beasts on the farms of Ireland are the birds that fly over them.

Many hundreds of people are destitute even of the very goods they possess.

Iron gates will last forever and afterwards they can be used for making horse shoes.

I answered in the affirmative with an emphatic 'No!'

Three-quarters of what the opposition says about us is lies and the other half is without any foundation in truth.

Mister Speaker, the country is in such a desperate state that little children, who can neither walk nor talk, are running around the streets cursing their maker.

The present tax on shoe leather is putting an intolerable burden on the bare-footed peasantry of Ireland.

I would give up half – nay, the whole of the constitution to preserve the remainder.

Single misfortunes rarely come alone and the worst of all misfortunes is usually followed by a greater misfortune.

The only way of preventing what is past is to put a stop to it before it happens.

The cup of Ireland's miseries has been overflowing for centuries, but it is not yet full.

I stand here, neither partial nor impartial.

Half the lies our opponents tell about us are not true.

I should have answered your letter a fortnight ago, but I didn't receive it until this morning.

While I write this I hold a sword in one hand and a pistol in the other.

Hal Roach

Have you been to Donegal? What a town. You plug in your shaver and the street lights dim.

You know it is summer in Ireland when the rain gets warmer.

The weather in Cork is something else. It's the only place in the world you can wake up in the morning and hear the birds coughing.

George Russell

A literary movement is five or six people who live in the same town and hate each other.

George Salmon

Mahaffy was caned only once in his life and that was for telling the truth – but it certainly cured him.

George Bernard Shaw

The British national anthem belongs to the eighteenth century. In it you find us ordering God about to do our political work.

The little I know, I owe to my ignorance.

A character actor is one who cannot act and therefore makes an elaborate study of disguise and stage tricks by which acting can be grotesquely simulated.

I am an unbeliever but I sometimes have doubts.

Certainly I enjoyed myself at your party. There was nothing else to enjoy.

I am informed that Lady Marlborough will be AT HOME on March 26th. So will I.

Who would I recommend to set *Pygmalion* to music? Mozart.

The Red Flag sounds like the funeral march of a fried eel.

Advice is like kissing. It costs nothing and it's a pleasant thing to do.

I have never been able to see how the duties of a critic, which consist largely in making painful remarks in public about the most sensitive of his fellow creatures, can be reconciled with the manners of a gentleman.

A man who has no office to go to – I don't care who he is – is a trial of which you can have no conception.

You don't expect me to know what to say about a play when I don't know who the author is, do you? If it's by a good author, it's a good play, naturally. That stands to reason.

Who is this Babe Ruth and what does she do?

Which painting in the National Gallery would I save if there was a fire? The one nearest the door of course.

He who can, does – he who cannot, teaches.

Only lawyers and mental defectives are automatically exempt from jury duty.

Two people getting together to write a book is like three people getting together to have a baby. One of them is superfluous.

Nature, not content with denying him the art of thinking, conferred on him the gift of writing.

I can forgive Alfred Nobel for having invented dynamite, but only a fiend in human form could have invented the Nobel prize.

I often quote myself. It adds spice to my conversations.

Condemned female murderers get sheaves of offers of marriage.

When we want to read about the deeds that are done for love, whither do we turn? To the murder columns.

A woman waits motionless until she is wooed. That is how the spider waits for the fly.

Animals are my friends – I do not eat my friends.

Communism is the lay form of Catholicism.

I was always unlawful; I broke the law when I was born because my parents weren't married.

Go on writing plays, my boy. One of these days a London producer will go into his office and say to his secretary, 'Is there a play from Shaw this morning?' and when she says 'No' he will say, 'Well, then we'll have to start on the rubbish.' And that's your chance, my boy.

First love is only a little foolishness and a lot of curiosity. No really self-respecting woman would take advantage of it.

The English churchgoer prefers a severe preacher because he thinks a few home truths will do his neighbour no harm.

An Englishman thinks he is being moral when he is only being uncomfortable.

Drink is the curse of my unhappy country. I take it myself because I have a weak heart and a poor digestion; but in principle I'm a teetotaller.

The man that is not prejudiced against a horse-thief is not fit to sit on a jury in this town.

Am I Shaw? I am positive.

Venus, a beautiful good-natured lady, was the goddess of love; Juno, a terrible shrew, the goddess of marriage; and they were always mortal enemies.

Marriage will always be a popular institution, because it combines a maximum of temptation with a maximum of opportunity.

I have a beard because I have written several plays in the time I would have spent shaving.

If all economists were laid end to end, they would not reach a conclusion.

Nobel Prize money is a lifebelt thrown to a swimmer who has already reached the shore safely.

A newspaper is a device which is unable to discriminate between a bicycle accident and the collapse of civilisation.

He knows nothing and thinks he knows everything. That points clearly to a political career.

Games are for people who can neither read nor think.

When men die of disease they are said to die of natural causes. When they recover (and they mostly do) the doctor gets the credit for curing them.

Nothing soothes me more after a long and maddening course of piano recitals than to sit and have my teeth drilled.

The British soldier can stand up to anything – except the British War Office.

There is no love sincerer than the love of food.

There is no satisfaction in hanging a man who does not object to it.

Lord Rosebery was a man who never missed an occasion to let slip an opportunity.

England and America are two countries separated by the same language.

Dancing is a perpendicular expression of a horizontal desire.

We were not fairly beaten. No Englishman is ever fairly beaten.

A drama critic is a man who leaves no turn unstoned.

Women want other women's husbands like horse-thieves prefer a horse that is broken in to one that is wild.

A man should have one woman to prevent him thinking too much about women in general.

Irish Protestantism is not a religion. It is a class prejudice, a conviction that Roman Catholics are socially inferior persons who will go to Hell when they die and leave Heaven in the exclusive possession of Protestant ladies and gentlemen.

The only man who had a proper understanding of Parliament was old Guy Fawkes.

A brigand lives by robbing the rich; a gentleman by robbing the poor.

Very nice sort of place, Oxford, I should think, for people who like that sort of place.

I am somewhat surprised to hear a Roman Catholic quote so essentially a Protestant document as the Bible.

A businessman is someone to whom age brings golf instead of wisdom.

I have never thought much of the courage of the lion-tamer; inside the cage he is at least safe from other men.

My father must have had some elementary education for he could read and write and keep accounts inaccurately.

If more than ten per cent of the population likes a painting it should be burned for it must be bad.

I came across a book I had signed 'With compliments' to a friend, in a second-hand bookshop. So I bought it and sent it to him signed 'With renewed compliments'.

Alcohol is an admirable commodity which enables Parliament to do things at eleven at night that no sane person would do at eleven in the morning.

Signor Tamerlik sings in a doubtful falsetto and his movements are unmeaning and frequently absurd. For the C sharp in the celebrated duet he substituted a strange description of shriek at about that pitch. The audience, ever appreciative of vocal curiosities, eagerly redemanded it.

There are just two classes in good society in England. The equestrian classes and the neurotic classes.

She had lost the art of conversation but not, unfortunately, the power of speech.

I believe in the discipline of silence and could talk for hours about it.

In baseball I see no reason why the infield should not try to put the batter off his stride at the critical moment by neatly timed disparagement of his mother's respectability.

I've posed nude for a photographer in the manner of Rodin's *Thinker*, but I looked merely constipated.

I am a teetotaller because my family has already paid its debt to the distilling industry so munificently as to leave me no further obligation.

The chief objection to playing wind instruments is that it prolongs the life of the player beyond all reasonable limits.

With regard to Gounod's *Redemption*, if you will only take the precaution to go in long enough after it commences and to come out long enough before it is over, you will not find it wearisome.

The French don't care what they do as long as they pronounce it properly.

Americans adore me and will go on adoring me until I say something nice about them.

I showed my appreciation of my native land in the usual way by getting out of it as soon as I possibly could.

An asylum for the sane would be empty in America.

We want a few mad people – look at where the sane ones have landed us.

It was not until I went back to Ireland as a tourist that I perceived the charm of my country was quite independent of my having been born in it.

The spectacle of twenty-two grown men with hairy legs chasing a bladder filled with air from one end of a field to another is both ludicrous and infantile.

Baseball has the advantage over cricket of being sooner ended.

The world contrived to get on before I was born (I don't quite know how) and I dare say it will make some sort of lame shift after I am dead.

Kings are not born; they are made by artificial hallucination.

A fool's brain digests philosophy into folly, science into superstition, and art into pedantry. Hence university education.

A woman seeking a husband is the most unscrupulous of all beasts of prey.

An actor who drinks is in a bad way; but the actor who eats is lost.

The natural term of the affection of the human animal for its offspring is six years.

Jim Sheridan

There's a great saying in Ireland, and it's not without irony. It says that the last time we played England we beat them one–all.

John D. Sheridan

The first rule of hospitality is that the visitor must never get a glimpse of the conditions in which you normally live.

I read where an ape has been taught to speak two words of English – when he learns ninety-eight more he can go to Hollywood and become a producer.

My soccer career was brief and inglorious. I played in only one match, and scored a goal with a brilliant left-footed drive that gave our goalkeeper no chance.

What prompted me to take up writing? Well, in the first place, the sandwich-board used to chafe me.

This book is dedicated to whom it may concern.

Once a woman has decided to knit a jersey, nothing short of total paralysis will stop her.

When you are putting well, you are a good putter; when your opponent is putting well, he has a good putter.

'Stance' is defined by the Rules of Golf as 'that which you have taken up when you place your feet on the ground in position for and preparatory to striking at the ball'. The location of the feet before they are placed on the ground is left to the discretion of the individual player.

When my wife is away and I am left to keep house for myself, I know it is time to do the washing-up when I put something on the kitchen table and something falls off the other end.

Richard Brinsley Sheridan

I find if I don't die in Autumn, I always seem to survive until Christmas.

I think the interpreter is the harder to understand of the two.

You must have women dressed, if it is only for the pleasure of imagining them as Venuses.

I handed one of my creditors an IOU and thought, thank God that's settled.

A wise woman will always let her husband have her way.

'Tis safest in matrimony to begin with a little aversion.

I refused to have an operation on the grounds that I already had two operations and found them painful. They were having my hair cut and sitting for a portrait.

She has a charming fresh colour, when it is fresh put on.

From the silence that prevails, I conclude that Lauderdale has been telling a joke.

It is not in my interest to pay the principal nor in my principle to pay the interest.

One would as soon make love to the Archbishop of Canterbury as to Mrs Siddons.

When a heroine goes mad, she always goes into white satin.

The right honourable gentleman is indebted to his memory for his jests, and to his imagination for his facts.

A Limerick banker had an iron leg and it was the softest thing about him.

My honourable friend has just gone to London with a shirt and a guinea and he'll not change either until he comes back.

She is as headstrong as an allegory on the banks of the Nile.

I would rather choose a wife of mine to have the usual number of limbs, and although one eye may be very agreeable, the prejudice has always run in favour of two.

When she has finished painting her face she joins it on so badly to her neck that she looks like a mended statue.

When my son Tom announced that he would proclaim his independence of party as an MP by writing the words TO LET on his forehead, I advised him to write underneath, UNFURNISHED.

Fergus Slattery

The motto of Irish rugby has always been 'Kick ahead, any head'.

James Stephens

Men come of age at sixty, women at sixteen.

Sleep is an excellent way of listening to the opera.

Jonathan Swift

He was a fiddler and consequently a rogue.

Steele might become a reasonably good writer if he would pay a little more attention to grammar, learn something about the propriety and disposition of words, and, incidentally, get some information on the subject he intends to handle.

Eleven men well armed will certainly subdue one single man in his shirt.

Whatever you say against women, they are better creatures than me, for men were made of clay, but woman was made of man.

As universal a practice as lying is, and as easy a one as it seems, I do not remember to have heard three good lies in any conversation, even from those who were most celebrated in that faculty.

I must go and do that which no one else can do for me.

In Church your grandsire cut his throat;
To do the job too long he tarried.
He should have had my hearty vote,
To cut his throat before he married.

A tavern is a place where they sell madness by the bottle.

If a lump of soot falls into the soup, and you cannot conveniently get it out, stir it well in, and it will give the soup a French taste.

No man is thoroughly miserable unless he is condemned to live in Ireland.

Why, every one as they like; as the good woman said when she kissed her cow.

Never remark in England that the air in Ireland is healthy and excellent or they will most certainly tax it.

Bring not a bagpipe to a man in trouble.

If the Church and the devil went to law the devil would win for all the lawyers and attorneys would be on his side.

I am almost done with harridans, and shall soon become old enough to fall in love with girls of fourteen.

I never knew any man in my life who could not bear another's misfortune perfectly like a Christian.

I propose that a tax be levied on female beauty. Let every woman be permitted to assess her own charms – then she'll be generous enough.

He had been eight years upon a project for extracting sunbeams out of cucumbers, which were to be put into phials hermetically sealed and let out to warm the air in raw inclement summers.

Under an oak in stormy weather,
I joined this rogue and whore together;
And none but he who rules the thunder
Can pull this rogue and whore asunder.

A man who had a mind to sell his house, carried a piece of brick in his pocket, which he showed as a pattern to encourage purchasers.

Faith, that's as well said, as if I had said it myself.

Servants, never come till you have been called
three or four times or more, for none but dogs will
come at the first whistle; and when the master
calls, 'Who's there?', no servant is bound to come;
for who's there is nobody's name.

Never lie to your master or mistress, unless you
have some hopes that they cannot find it out.

A very little wit is valued in a woman, as we are
pleased with a few words spoken plain by a parrot.

All political parties die of swallowing their own
lies.

I have been assured by a very knowing American of my acquaintance in London that a healthy young child, well nursed, is at a year old a most delicious, nourishing and wholesome food, whether steamed, roasted, baked or boiled: and I make no doubt that it will equally serve in a fricassee or a ragout.

You have a head, and so has a pin.

Servants never come till you have been called three or four times or more, for none but dogs will come at the first whistle; and when the master calls, 'Who's there?', no servant is bound to come; for who's there is nobody's name.

J. M. Synge.

I don't know if he is dead or not, but they took the liberty of burying him.

Dennis Taylor

Alex Higgins should have been here today, but he was launching a ship in Belfast and they couldn't get him to let go of the bottle.

They say the situation in Northern Ireland is not as bad as they say it is.

Niall Toibín

We are now approaching Belfast Airport. Please fasten your seatbelts, extinguish your cigarettes and put your watches back three hundred years.

A restaurant I used to frequent in Cork advertised 'Eat here and you'll never eat anywhere else again.'

Gary Cooper had two emotions: 'hat on' and 'hat off'.

The man was a secular version of the Immaculate Conception: he became an alcoholic without ever buying a drink.

The Irish equivalent of 'gilding the lily' can be translated as 'rubbing lard on a sow's arse'.

The true Dubliner is a man who can peel an orange in his pocket.

A Cavan farmer, to cover the possibility of sudden unexpected visitors, can often be found eating his dinner from a drawer.

People from the Irish Midlands are often described as 'phlegmatic' which is another word for 'thick'.

An Irishman is just a machine for turning Guinness into urine, which as any Murphy's drinker will tell you is a superfluous exercise anyway.

Joe Tomelty

If there is music in Hell it will be bagpipes.

Eric Tully

He was a unique man and unique men are rare.

George Tyrrell

A Temperance Hotel! You might as well talk about a celibate brothel.

I never quite forgave Mahaffy for getting himself suspended from preaching in the College Chapel.

Ever since his sermons were discontinued, I suffer from insomnia in church.

Mervyn Wall

The odour of sanctity was clearly discernible from his breath and person.

Tony Ward

The garryowen in rugby is basically a Hail Mary kick – send it up to Heaven and hope for the best.

Duke of Wellington

I don't know what effect those men will have on the enemy, but, by God, they terrify me.

I can only hope that when the enemy reads the list of my officers' names he trembles as I do.

Just because a racehorse is born in a pigsty, that does not make him a pig.

God save the Queen, and may all your wives be like her.

The Irish militia are useless in times of war, and dangerous in times of peace.

We always have been, we are and I hope that we always shall be, detested in France.

What would I like the sermon to be about, vicar? I would like it to be about ten minutes.

I am, sir, your humble and obedient servant, which you know, and I know, is a damned lie.

The first Reformed Parliament – I never saw so many shocking bad hats in my life.

Oscar Wilde

I do not in any way approve of the modern sympathy with invalids. I consider it morbid. Illness of any kind is hardly a thing to be encouraged in others.

Thinking is the most unhealthy thing in the world and people die of it just as they die of any other disease. Fortunately, in England at any rate, thought is not catching.

Frank Harris is upstairs thinking about Shakespeare at the top of his voice.

The advantage of the emotions is that they lead us astray.

Life is one fool thing after another, whereas love is two fool things after each other.

One should never listen. To listen is a sign of indifference to one's hearers.

No gentleman ever has any money and no gentleman ever takes exercise.

The view from a hotel room is immaterial except to the hotelier, who of course charges it on the bill. A gentleman never looks out of the window.

The performance of the *Three Musketeers* was Athos, Pathos and Bathos.

The Alps are objects of appallingly bad taste.

When can one love someone truly? Only when one is safely married and then with the greatest discretion.

It is always a silly thing to give advice but to give good advice is absolutely fatal.

The Atlantic Ocean was disappointing.

Details are always vulgar.

The art of conversation is really within the reach of almost everyone, except those who are morbidly truthful.

I detest games – I never like to kick or be kicked.

I want to introduce you to my mother. We have founded a society for the suppression of virtue.

Psychology is in its infancy as a science. I hope, in the interests of art, it will always remain so.

The conscience of an editor is purely decorative.

Nobody, not even in the provinces, should ever be allowed to ask an intelligent question about pure mathematics across a dinner table.

To disagree with three-fourths of the British public on all points is one of the first elements of sanity, one of the deepest consolations in all moments of spiritual doubt.

There are moments when art almost attains the dignity of manual labour.

My first idea was to print only three copies of my poem; one for myself, one for the British Museum, and one for Heaven. I had some doubt about the British Museum.

On the staircase stood several Royal Academicians, disguised as artists.

Knight's biography of Rossetti is just the sort of biography Guildenstern might have written of Hamlet.

Examinations are pure humbug from beginning to end. If a man is a gentleman, he knows quite enough, and if he is not a gentleman, whatever he knows is bad for him.

Many a young man starts in life with a natural gift which, if nurtured in congenial and sympathetic surroundings, or by imitation of the best models, might grow into something really great and wonderful. But, as a rule, he comes to nothing. He either falls into careless habits of accuracy or takes to frequenting the society of the aged and the well-informed, and in a short time he develops a morbid and unhealthy faculty of truth-telling.

The only way a woman can ever reform a man is by boring him so completely that he loses all possible interest in life.

I am due at the club. It is the hour when we sleep there.

Originality is no longer possible, even in sin.

Chicken? Why do you give me these pedestrians to eat?

Astray by Charlotte M.Yonge and three other writers needed four people to write it and even to read it requires assistance; all the same it is a book that one can with perfect safety recommend to other people.

I don't have any religion – I am an Irish Protestant.

He never touches water. It goes to his head at once.

With an evening coat and a white tie, anybody, even a stockbroker, can gain a reputation for being civilised.

Why does not science, instead of troubling itself about sunspots, which nobody ever saw, or, if they did see, ought not to speak about, busy itself with drainage and sanitary engineering?

The basis of action is a lack of imagination. It is the last resource of those who know not how to dream.

Intuition is the strange instinct that tells a woman she is right, whether she is or not.

I can't remember your name. But don't tell me.

I think it is so kind of the mimic to tell us who he is imitating. It avoids discussion, doesn't it?

I used to go to the office three times a week for an hour a day, but I have since struck off one of the days.

The Catholic Church is for saints and sinners. For respectable people the Anglican Church will do.

In the United States of America there are no trappings, no pageants. I saw only two processions: one was the Fire Brigade preceded by the Police and the other was the Police preceded by the Fire Brigade.

I am a man of regular habits. I am always in bed by four or five.

Zola is determined to show that, if he has not got genius, he can at least be dull. And how well he succeeds!

I suppose publishers are untrustworthy. They always certainly look it.

I know so many men in London whose only talent is for washing. I suppose that is why men of genius so seldom wash; they are afraid of being mistaken for men of talent only.

Do not be led astray into the paths of virtue.

Anything becomes a pleasure if one does it too often.

The only way to atone for being occasionally a little over-dressed is by being always absolutely over-educated.

The only possible form of exercise is to talk, not to walk.

She is a peacock in everything but beauty.

Nothing makes one so vain as being told that one is a sinner.

Woman's first duty is to her dressmaker. What her second duty is no one has yet discovered.

The title of my next book is *Are the Commentators on Hamlet Really Mad or Only Pretending to Be?*

Arthur Pinero's play is the best I have ever slept through.

Anybody can act. Most people in England do nothing else.

Perhaps it is true that dramatic critics can be bought, but, judging from their appearance, most of them cannot be at all expensive.

I was in hopes that Lord Illingworth would have married Lady Kelso. But I believe he said her family was too large. Or was it her feet? I forget which.

The street was in a rough neighbourhood. It was near the Houses of Parliament.

It is indeed a burning shame that there should be one law for men and another law for women. I think there should be no law for anybody.

Thank heaven there are no nightingales in the countryside to ruin the music of the stillness with their well-meant but ill-produced voices.

Switzerland has produced nothing except theologians and waiters.

At the holy season of Easter one is supposed to forgive all one's friends.

It is much easier for a Scotsman to be a genius than to be an artist.

Finding that the Vatican Gardens were open only to Bohemian and Portuguese pilgrims, I at once spoke both languages fluently, explaining that my English dress was a form of penance.

I cannot stand Christians because they are never Catholics and I cannot stand Catholics because they are never Christians. Otherwise I am at one with the Indivisible Church.

In March 1893 I took rooms at the Savoy Hotel and often spent the night there. I could not go home as I had forgotten the number of my house and I was not quite certain of the street, though I believe the district was Chelsea.

In prison I studied German. Indeed, this seems to be the proper place for such study.

Dissatisfied with the faith, I took up photography, at which I became so good that in moments of depression I felt I was a born photographer. Tiring of churches, I tried cows, and I discovered with pleasure that cows are very fond of being photographed, and, unlike architecture, don't move.

We do not go to war with France because her prose is perfect.

We must present ourselves at Holloway Gaol at four o'clock. After that it is difficult to gain admission.

Varnishing is the only artistic process with which the Royal Academicians are thoroughly familiar.

I have made an important discovery: that alcohol, taken in sufficient quantities, produces all the effects of intoxication.

No modern literary work of any worth has been produced in the English language by an English writer – except, of course, Bradshaw [author of railway timetables]

To give an accurate description of what never happened is the proper occupation of the historian.

In luncheon parties in old days, the remains of the guests were taken away with the debris of the feast.

The Chronicle of Mites is a mock-heroic poem about the inhabitants of a decaying cheese who speculate about the origin of their species and hold learned discussions upon the meaning of evolution and the Gospel according to Darwin. This cheese-epic is a rather unsavoury production and the style is at times so monstrous and so realistic that the author should be called the Gorgon-Zola of literature.

I cannot choose one hundred best books because I have written only five.

My talent I put into my writing, my genius I have saved for living.

This verse has all the ring of Macaulay in it, and is a form of poetry which cannot possibly harm anybody, even if translated into French.

There must be five hundred signed copies for particular friends; six for the general public; and one for America.

Why was I born with such contemporaries?

There seems to be some curious connection between piety and poor rhymes.

All the good things in life are immoral, illegal, or heavily taxed.

Few parents nowadays pay any regard to what their children say to them. The old-fashioned respect for the young is fast dying out.

I have little experience of marriage, having been married only once.

Women represent the triumph of matter over mind, just as men represent the triumph of mind over morals.

The happiness of a married man depends on the people he has not married.

Women delight in men over seventy. They offer one the devotion of a lifetime.

The real drawback of marriage is that it makes one unselfish.

When you convert someone to an idea, you lose faith in it.

To be natural is such a very difficult pose to keep up.

I suppose I could make changes in my play but who am I to tamper with a masterpiece?

It's a terrible thing for a man to find out suddenly that all his life he has been speaking nothing but the truth.

To get into the best society nowadays, one has either to feed people, amuse people, or shock people.

Insincerity is merely a method whereby we can multiply our personalities.

I can sympathise with everything, except suffering.

W. E. Henley has fought the good fight and has had to face every difficulty except popularity.

To many no doubt, he will seem blatant and bumptious, but we prefer to regard him as being simply British.

Duty is what one expects from others, it is not what one does oneself.

You seem quite out of sorts. You haven't quarrelled with your cook, I hope? What a tragedy that would be for you; you would lose all your friends.

The only thing that sustains one through life is the consciousness of the immense inferiority of everybody else, and this is a feeling I have always cultivated.

The music is in German. You would not understand it.

Charity creates a multitude of sins.

Mamma, whose views on education are remarkably strict, has brought me up to be extremely short-sighted; it is part of her system.

A cheque is the only argument I recognise.

Good heavens! How marriage ruins a man! It's as demoralising as cigarettes and far more expensive.

His work was that curious mixture of bad painting and good intentions that always entitles a man to be called a representative British artist.

The baby is wonderful: it has a bridge to its nose which the nurse says is a proof of genius! It also has a superb voice, which it freely exercises: its style is essentially Wagnerian.

There is much to be said in favour of modern journalism. By giving us the opinions of the uneducated, it keeps us in touch with the ignorance of the community.

Somebody must listen, and I like to do all the talking myself. It saves time and prevents arguments.

The chapter on the fall of the Rupee you may omit. It is somewhat sensational.

It is always painful to part from people whom one has known for a very brief space of time. The absence of old friends one can endure with equanimity.

One should never make one's debut with a scandal. One should reserve that to give an interest to one's old age.

The best one can say of most modern creative art is that it is just a little less vulgar than reality.

Mr Hall Caine writes at the top of his voice.

An unbiased opinion is always absolutely valueless.

Never trust a woman who wears mauve, whatever her age may be, or a woman over thirty-five who is fond of pink ribbons. It always means they have a history.

It is an odd thing, but everyone who disappears is said to be seen in San Francisco. It must be a delightful city and possess all the attractions of the next world.

Fathers should be neither seen nor heard. That is the only proper basis for family life.

Excuse me, I didn't recognise you. I've changed so much.

There are terrible temptations that it requires strength and courage to yield to.

Some cause happiness wherever they go; others whenever they go.

Looking good and dressing well are essential. A purpose in life is not.

Religion is the fashionable substitute for belief.

Mr Whistler has always spelled art with a capital 'I'.

It is better to have a permanent income than to be fascinating.

Anyone who lives within their means suffers from a lack of imagination.

After a good dinner, one can forgive anybody, even one's own relations.

One never trusts anyone that one has deceived.

Niagara Falls is simply a vast unnecessary amount of water going the wrong way and then falling over unnecessary rocks.

One half of the world does not believe in God and the other half does not believe in me.

Fashion is what one wears oneself.

A well-tied tie is the first serious step in life.

Philanthropy is the refuge of people who wish to annoy their fellow creatures.

My dear delightful company, I have just watched your performance of *The Importance of Being Earnest*. It reminded me of a play I once wrote.

Whenever people talk to me about the weather, I always feel certain that they mean something else.

Other people are quite dreadful. The only possible society is oneself.

Work is the refuge of people who have nothing better to do.

Gold-tipped cigarettes are awfully expensive; I can afford them only when I am in debt.

Rich bachelors should be taxed. It is not fair that some men should be happier than others.

Half the success of Marie Corelli is due to the no doubt unfounded rumour that she is a woman.

George Moore leads his readers to the latrine and locks them in.

I like Wagner's music better than anybody's. It is so loud that one can talk the whole time without other people hearing what one says.

Of course, if one had enough money to go to America, one wouldn't go.

Herbert Beerbohm Tree is a charming fellow, and so clever; he models himself on me.

A true friend does not stab you in the back, he stabs you in the front.

Mr Whistler, with all his faults, was never guilty of writing a line of poetry.

The only thoroughly original ideas I have ever heard Mr Whistler express have had reference to his superiority as a painter over painters greater than himself.

When I was young I used to think that money was the most important thing in life. Now that I am old, I know it is.

It is only by not paying one's bills that one can hope to live in the memory of the commercial classes.

Ignorance is like a delicate exotic fruit; touch it and the bloom is gone.

Whenever cannibals are on the brink of starvation, Heaven, in its infinite mercy, sends them a fat missionary.

Tell the cook of this restaurant with my compliments that these are the very worst sandwiches in the whole world, and that, when I ask for a watercress sandwich, I do not mean a loaf with a field in the middle of it.

I often take exercise. Why only yesterday I had breakfast in bed.

I never travel without my diary. One should always have something sensational to read on the train.

I was working on the proofs of one of my poems all day. In the morning I put a comma in and in the afternoon I took it back out again.

I've given up reading books. I find it takes my mind off myself.

Work is the curse of the drinking classes.

There are two ways of disliking poetry. One way is to dislike it and the other is to read Pope.

This book of Italian literature shows a want of knowledge that must be the result of years of study.

One should not be too severe on English novels; they are the only relaxation of the intellectually unemployed.

The General was essentially a man of peace – except of course in his domestic affairs.

To lose one parent may be regarded as a misfortune; to lose both looks like carelessness.

Andiatorocte is the title of a volume of poems by the Rev. Clarence Walworth of Albany, NY. It is a word borrowed from the Indians and should, we think, be returned to them as soon as possible.

There is nothing in the world like the devotion of a married woman. It's a thing no married man knows anything about.

Niagara Falls is the bride's second great disappointment.

Women have a much better time than men in this world. There are far more things forbidden to them.

Women love men for their defects; if men have enough of them, women will forgive them everything, even their gigantic intellects.

Dammit, sir, it is your duty to get married. You can't always be living for pleasure.

Poor old Lord Mortlake, who had only two topics of conversation; his gout and his wife. I never could quite make out which of the two he was talking about.

Please do not shoot the pianist – he is doing his best.

As for marriage, it is one of America's most popular institutions. The American man marries early and the American woman marries often; and they get on extremely well together.

You must play Chopin to me. The man with whom my wife ran away played Chopin exquisitely.

Of course America had often been discovered
before Columbus, but it had always been hushed
up.

I have to choose between this world, the next
world and Australia.

Know him? I know him so well that we haven't
spoken to each other for over ten years.

Always forgive your enemies. Nothing annoys
them so much.

If this is the way that Queen Victoria treats her
prisoners, she doesn't deserve to have any.

I must decline your invitation owing to an
engagement I am just about to make.

It is perfectly monstrous the way people go about nowadays saying things against one, behind one's back, that are absolutely and entirely true.

I always pass on good advice – it's the only thing one can do with it.

It is very easy to endure the difficulties of one's enemies. It is the successes of one's friends that are hard to bear.

Frank Harris has been invited to every great house in England – once.

I can resist everything except temptation.

Fashion is a form of ugliness so intolerable that we have to alter it every six months.

I live in terror of not being misunderstood.

You should study the Peerage; it is the best thing in fiction the English have ever done.

The extraordinary thing about the lower classes in England is that they are always losing their relations. They are extremely fortunate in that respect.

The English country gentleman galloping after a fox – the unspeakable in pursuit of the uneatable.

A cigarette is the perfect type of a perfect pleasure. It is exquisite and leaves one quite unsatisfied. What more can one want?

I can believe anything as long as it is incredible.

Thirty-five is a very attractive age. London society is full of women who have of their own free choice remained thirty-five for years.

Football is all very well – a good game for rough girls, but not for delicate boys.

One should always play fairly when one has the winning cards.

I never play cricket. It requires one to assume such indecent postures.

The play was a great success, but the audience was a disaster.

The English public takes no interest in a work of art until it is told that the work in question is immoral.

A plagiarist is a writer of plays.

A gentleman never insults anyone unintentionally.

One can survive anything nowadays except death and live down anything except a good reputation.

If one hears bad music it is one's duty to drown it by one's conversation.

I don't want money. It is only people who pay their bills who want money and I never pay mine.

Meredith is a prose Browning, and so is Browning.

There is only one thing worse than being talked about and that is not being talked about.

I hate vulgar realism in literature. The man who would call a spade a spade should be compelled to use one. It is the only thing he is fit for.

Bernard Shaw is an excellent man; he has not an enemy in the world and none of his friends like him.

When I was your age I had been an inconsolable widower for three months, and was already paying my addresses to your admirable mother.

When I went to America, I had two secretaries – one for autographs, the other for locks of hair. Within six months the one had died of writer's cramp, the other was completely bald.

Long engagements give people the opportunity of finding out each other's character before marriage, which is never advisable.

An engagement is hardly a serious one that has not been broken off at least once.

I sometimes think that God in creating man somewhat overestimated His ability.

It is only an auctioneer who can equally and impartially admire all schools of art.

Bad artists always admire each other's work; they call it being broadminded and free from prejudice.

Friendship is far more tragic than love. It lasts longer.

When you are alone with Max Beerbohm, he takes off his face and reveals his mask.

He knew the precise psychological moment when to say nothing.

Punctuality is the thief of time.

I have nothing to declare except my genius.

George Moore wrote excellent English until he discovered grammar.

To win back my youth there is nothing I won't do – except to take exercise, get up early and be a useful member of the community.

I don't at all like knowing what people say of me behind my back. It makes me far too conceited.

Meredith! Who can define him? His style is chaos illuminated by flashes of lightning. As a writer he has mastered everything except language: as a novelist he can do everything except tell a story. As an artist he is everything, except articulate.

Being natural is only a pose, and the most irritating pose I know.

In England, at any rate, education produces no effect whatsoever. If it did, it would prove a serious danger to the upper classes, and would probably lead to acts of violence in Grosvenor Square.

If one tells the truth, one is sure, sooner or later, to be found out.

In examinations, the foolish ask questions that the wise cannot answer.

The old believe everything: the middle-aged
suspect everything: the young know everything.

Everybody who is incapable of learning has taken
to teaching.

Morality is simply the attitude we adopt towards
people whom we personally dislike.

In married life, three is company and two is none.

Untruthful! My nephew, Algernon? Impossible!
He is an Oxonian.

No woman should ever be quite accurate about
her age. It looks so calculating.

No good deed ever goes unpunished.

I hear her hair has turned quite gold from grief.

John Winstanley

Cries Celia to a reverend dean
'What reason can be given
Since marriage is a holy thing,
That there are none in heaven?'

'There are no women,' he replied;
She quick returned the jest;
'Women there are, but I'm afraid,
They cannot find a priest.'

Gordon Wood

The Irish Rugby team in my day was all boot,
bollock and bite.

John Butler Yeats

A man who understands one woman is qualified to understand pretty well everything.

William Butler Yeats

I am not feeling very well. I can only write prose today.

Some people say there is a God; others say there is no God. The truth probably lies somewhere in between.

The only trouble with Seamus O'Sullivan is that when he's not drunk he's sober.

I know I have won the Nobel Prize for Literature. Stop babbling man – how much?

Dublin's O'Connell Street contains statues of
Daniel O'Connell, Charles Stewart Parnell and
Lord Nelson – three of history's best-known
adulterers.

If the English could only learn to believe in fairies,
there wouldn't ever have been any Irish problem.

What They Say about the Irish

Rowan Atkinson

The first commandment of life in Ireland would appear to be, thou shalt never under any circumstances wash a car.

Jo Brand

I like the Irish but I cannot quite understand how when I say, 'I'm from London,' in a Dublin pub, this tends to be heard as, 'I am Oliver Cromwell.'

George Carlin

My father was from Donegal – he didn't metabolise ethanol very well.

Quentin Crisp

When I told the people of Northern Ireland that I was an atheist, a woman in the audience stood up and asked if it was the Catholic God or the Protestant God I didn't believe in.

J. P. Donleavy

When I die I want to decompose in a barrel of porter and have it served in all the pubs in Dublin.

Kenneth Fraser

I never met anyone in Ireland who understood the Irish question; except one Englishman who had been there only a week.

Sigmund Freud

The Irish are one race of people for whom psychoanalysis is of no use whatsoever.

Oliver Herford

The Irish gave the bagpipes to the Scots as a joke, but the Scots haven't seen the joke yet.

Samuel Johnson

The Irish are a fair people – they never speak well of one another.

Dublin, though a place much worse than London, is not so bad as Iceland.

Sidney Littlewood

The Irish don't know what they want and are prepared to fight to the death to get it.

Patrick Murray

God created alcohol just to stop the Irish from ruling the world.

Only one arrest was made at the Belgium v. Ireland match in Brussels. It was an Irishman with a painted moustache who attempted to kiss a police horse.

The Irish are excellent timekeepers because they are used to working with watches that are an hour fast and ten minutes slow.

Austin O'Malley

God is good to the Irish, but no one else is, not even the Irish.

Eugene O'Neill

When St Patrick drove the snakes out of Ireland, they swam to New York and joined the police force.

Jeff Probyn

The Irish treat you like royalty before and after a game and kick you to pieces during it.

Will Rogers

The English should give Ireland Home Rule and reserve the motion picture rights.

Barry Took

In Ireland schizophrenics are treated not by one psychiatrist but two.

Mark Twain

Give an Irishman lager for a month, and he's a dead man. An Irishman is lined with copper and the beer corrodes it. But whiskey polishes the copper and is the saving of him.